Endorsements

"Christians are pressed by very real questions. How does Scripture structure a church, order worship, organize ministry, and define biblical leadership? Those are just examples of the questions that are answered clearly, carefully, and winsomely in this new series from 9Marks. I am so thankful for this ministry and for its incredibly healthy and hopeful influence in so many faithful churches. I eagerly commend this series."

R. Albert Mohler Jr., President, The Southern Baptist Theological Seminary

"Sincere questions deserve thoughtful answers. If you're not sure where to start in answering these questions, let this series serve as a diving board into the pool. These minibooks are winsomely to-the-point and great to read together with one friend or one hundred friends."

Gloria Furman, author, *Missional Motherhood* and *The Pastor's Wife*

"As a pastor, I get asked lots of questions. I'm approached by unbelievers seeking to understand the gospel, new believers unsure about next steps, and maturing believers wanting help answering questions from their Christian family, friends, neighbors, or coworkers. It's in these moments that I wish I had a book to give them that was brief, answered their questions, and pointed them in the right direction for further study. Church Questions is a series that provides just that. Each booklet tackles one question in a biblical, brief, and practical manner. The series may be called Church Questions, but it could be called 'Church Answers.' I intend to pick these up by the dozens and give them away regularly. You should too."

Juan R. Sanchez, Senior Pastor, High Pointe Baptist Church, Austin, Texas

"Where can we Christians find reliable answers to our common questions about life together at church—without having to plow through long, expensive books? The Church Questions booklets meet our need with answers that are biblical, thoughtful, and practical. For pastors, this series will prove a trustworthy resource for guiding church members toward deeper wisdom and stronger unity."

Ray Ortlund, President, Renewal Ministries

How Can
I Find Someone
to Disciple Me?

Church Questions

How Can
I Find Someone
to Disciple Me?

J. Garrett Kell

WHEATON, ILLINOIS

How Can I Find Someone to Disciple Me?

Copyright © 2021 by 9Marks

Published by Crossway
        1300 Crescent Street
        Wheaton, Illinois 60187

Cover design: Jordan Singer

First printing 2021

Printed in the United States of America

Trade paperback ISBN: 978-1-4335-7239-5
ePub ISBN: 978-1-4335-7240-1
PDF ISBN: 978-1-4335-7242-5
Mobipocket ISBN: 978-1-4335-7241-8

Library of Congress Cataloging-in-Publication Data

Names: Kell, J. Garrett, author.
Title: How can I find someone to disciple me? / J. Garrett Kell.
Description: Wheaton, Illinois : Crossway, 2021. | Series: Church questions |
    Includes bibliographical references and index.
Identifiers: LCCN 2020028965 (print) | LCCN 2020028966 (ebook) | ISBN
    9781433572395 (trade paperback) | ISBN 9781433572425 (pdf) | ISBN
    9781433572418 (mobi) | ISBN 9781433572401 (epub)
Subjects: LCSH: Discipling (Christianity) | Spiritual formation.
Classification: LCC BV4520 .K35 2021 (print) | LCC BV4520 (ebook) | DDC
    248.4—dc23
LC record available at https://lccn.loc.gov/2020028965
LC ebook record available at https://lccn.loc.gov/2020028966

Crossway is a publishing ministry of Good News Publishers.

BP		30	29	28	27	26	25	24	23	22	21
15	14	13	12	11	10	9	8	7	6	5	4	3	2	1

Be imitators of me, as I am of Christ.

1 Corinthians 11:1

Lord, bring me someone to help me follow you.

I didn't know what I was asking for, but I needed help.

Jesus invaded my life during my junior year of college and turned my world upside down. Weekends shifted from all-night raves to reading Scripture by myself. I attended church and met new friends. God was changing me, but I was riding a spiritual roller coaster. Sometimes I felt close to God, other times I was confused and uncertain how to follow him. I loved reading the Bible but often didn't understand it. I wanted my old friends to know Jesus, but occasionally

I'd join them in sin. I hated the struggle. I didn't know what to do.

So I prayed, *Lord, bring me someone to help me follow you.*

And God answered.

Shelby heard about my new faith in Jesus and took me out for tacos.[1] He asked questions about my life. He explained the Bible to me. He pointed out Romans 13:14 and challenged me, "Don't give the devil a chance. If you put yourself in tempting situations, you're more likely to fall into sin. Stay close to Jesus, and he'll protect you." I still remember that conversation over twenty years later. We met nearly every week that semester. He showed me how to follow Jesus.

Since that day, God has continually answered my prayer by sending me people who help me follow Jesus. Tommy showed me how to study the Bible. Gene displayed hospitality. Lisa modeled how to sing from the soul. Reid pressed me toward holiness. Mama Ruth embodied thankfulness. John taught me how to apply God's grace to brokenness. Beth showed me servanthood. Mark modeled humble leadership.

Each of these brothers and sisters, and many more, have taught me how to follow Jesus. Few things have strengthened my walk with Jesus like these discipling relationships.

This little booklet is written to help you find someone to disciple you—and prepare you to disciple others. But before we get too far along, let's answer two questions: (1) What is a disciple? and (2) What is discipling?

What Is a Disciple?

Most simply, a disciple is a follower. Disciples follow, learn from, and imitate someone else.

Christians are disciples of Jesus. He left us an example that we should follow (1 Pet. 2:21). We follow him by learning who he is, imitating his example, and obeying his commands.

Jesus calls us to be his disciple in passages like Luke 9:23–27:

> If anyone would come after me, let him deny himself and take up his cross daily

11

and follow me. For whoever would save
his life will lose it, but whoever loses his
life for my sake will save it. For what does
it profit a man if he gains the whole world
and loses or forfeits himself? For whoever
is ashamed of me and of my words, of him
will the Son of Man be ashamed when he
comes in his glory and the glory of the Father and of the holy angels.

Jesus's disciples have repented of sin, for-
saken the world, and committed their life to
follow him by faith. Jesus's disciples deny their
sinful desires through the power of the Holy
Spirit in order to please their Lord. Jesus's disciples daily lay down their lives for his name's
sake. Jesus's disciples know a day of judgment
is coming and strive to live every moment in
light of that day.

When Jesus calls someone to be his disciple,
he isn't simply calling him or her to join a club
or be part of a weird religious subculture. He's
calling them to turn from their sin and love
him every day until they see him face-to-face.

Being a disciple of Jesus isn't a one-time decision—it's an ongoing relationship. Each day we draw upon his grace and strive to live in obedience to him.

What Is Discipling?

Forty days after Jesus rose from the dead, he assembled his disciples and gave this commission:

> All authority in heaven and on earth has been given to me. Go therefore and make disciples of all nations, baptizing them in the name of the Father and of the Son and of the Holy Spirit, teaching them to observe all that I have commanded you. And behold, I am with you always, to the end of the age. (Matt. 28:18–20)

Jesus instructs his disciples that wherever they go, they must keep it as their main aim to "make disciples."

There are two aspects to disciple making.

First, we make disciples by calling people who don't follow Jesus to follow him. This is called evangelism. We proclaim the good news that Jesus died on the cross for sinners like us, and three days later he rose from the dead. We assure them that if they turn away from their sin and believe in him, he will forgive all their sins and reconcile them to God. If they respond rightly, they become Jesus's disciples.

Second, we make disciples by helping people who already know Jesus to grow in their relationship with him. We purposely do spiritual good to them. We help them obey all that Jesus commanded (Matt. 28:20). We teach people how to obey Jesus with their words, their work, their time, their money, their sexuality, and everything else you can think of. Jesus is the Lord over our whole lives, and everything we do should be aimed at pleasing him (2 Cor. 5:9; Eph. 5:10; Col. 1:10; 1 John 3:22).

If you're a disciple, then you should help others follow Jesus. You should also look for others to help you follow him too.

If you're reading this booklet, I assume you're ready to jump into a discipling relationship. In the pages ahead, we'll consider how you can find someone—or, even better, several people—to help you faithfully follow Jesus.

How Can I Find Someone to Disciple Me?

Finding someone to disciple you isn't complex, but it requires effort. Often, *you* will need to initiate the relationship. But trust that God will use every part of the discipling process, including finding discipling relationships, to deepen your dependence upon him.

Pray

God is our heavenly Father. He cares for us and wants us to trust him to supply everything we need. He promises to provide food and clothing (Matt 6:11, 25–33), rewards for good works (Matt. 6:4, 6, 18), wisdom in our suffering (James 1:5), and protection from temptation (Matt. 6:13). Jesus taught that God "knows what you need before you ask him" (Matt. 6:8). If God cares this much about you, don't you think he desires to bring you someone to help you walk with him? Ask God to provide discipling relationships. Keep asking him. Keep seeking His provision through faith-filled prayer. Because he is good, he will answer you (Matt. 7:7–11).

So what should you pray?

Pray to meet someone. Cornelius was a righteous man who desired to know God more (Acts 10). God heard his prayers and arranged for the Apostle Peter to visit him. Peter taught him about Jesus, and Cornelius, along with his entire family, believed the gospel. God is able to set up divine appointments and arrange circumstances so that you meet the right person to help you walk with him.

Pray for a humble spirit. It's time to ask yourself "do I *really* want to be discipled?" Following Jesus requires change. If someone is going to disciple you, you're going to need humility. Are you ready to be instructed? Do you want someone to point out your sins? Are you ready for correction and training? Pray for a humble, hopeful, teachable spirit so you can be ready to grow with God.

Pray to help someone else. As you seek someone to disciple you, ask God to use you to disciple others. Be on the lookout for people you can spiritually help. You may not feel you have much to offer others, but that's not true. If you're a Christian, you have God's Spirit and can bless others (Rom. 15:14; 1 Cor. 12:14–19). Who are new believers you can encourage in their walk with God? Who is someone you can read the Bible with? Who is someone you can do evangelism with? Prayerfully ask God to bring you someone you can help—and then go actively look for that person. One thing that you'll learn is, discipleship is almost never one way. The discipler often learns much from the disciple because every member of the body of Christ has something to contribute. Speaking of the body of Christ, the local church is the primary way God intends for his children to be discipled. Let's consider how.

Join a Church

As a young Christian I viewed church as optional. I was content reading the Bible on my own and attending whatever study or church service seemed best at the time. But I missed something important. God wants each of his children to grow up in a family—a local church filled with brothers and sisters who love, serve, encourage, and watch over one another. I needed to commit to fellow believers and build up their faith while being built up by them.

If you want to find someone to disciple you, join a church. After all, that's where God's people are. No perfect church exists but healthy churches do. Look for a church that preaches sermons from the Bible, regularly reminds you of God's grace in the gospel, stirs your love for Jesus, is a vibrant community of Christians, and has leadership whose faith is worthy of imitation.

The local church is the primary place you'll learn to obey Jesus's commands. As you lock arms with God's people, you'll learn to serve others, practice hospitality, apply the gospel to others, receive correction, forgive others when wronged, and love others as Christ has loved you (John 13:34–35). The local church is a discipling greenhouse. We gather to help one another fol-

low Jesus better and hold one another accountable as we seek to serve the Lord.

When we join a church, we're *committing* to
discipling relationships. The local church provides us with dozens of brothers or sisters who
each have something unique to teach us about
following Christ. Remember, you don't just need
one person discipling you, you need an entire
community teaching you to follow Jesus. Every
part needs every other part (1 Cor. 12:14–26).

Once you join a church, let me offer a few
additional pieces of advice about how to pursue
discipling relationships.

First, regularly gather with the church. Guard
your schedule to ensure nothing conflicts with
attending church on Sunday. Regularly assem-
bling with the church is an essential part of following Jesus (Heb. 10:24–25). Attend in faith.
Expect God to use his word and his people to
help you follow him. It may feel uncomfortable
at first, but over time, God will increase your
love for his church.

*Second, pursue relationships with fellow
church members.* Consistently gathering with

God's people will also help you build relationships with other members. You won't get to know folks if you only see them a few times every few months. But if you're rubbing shoulders with the same people each week, you'll more quickly develop friendships. Often, the best discipling relationships will emerge from our friendships with other church members.

Let's think about that last sentence a bit more. Discipling happens in both formal and informal contexts. Sometimes you may meet with an older saint and ask him for formal instruction on a particular issue. More often, meaningful discipling relationships will simply emerge as you spend time with friends in your local congregation. As you discuss parenting, evangelism, Scripture, or any other part of life, you'll be instructing one another and building one another up in the faith—even if you aren't formally meeting for a discipling session.

In fact, the beauty of the local church is that we're all helping one another follow Jesus. Younger saints even help more mature ones in their walk with the Lord. Just consider what Paul wrote to the church at Rome: "I long to see you, that I may impart to you some spiritual gift to strengthen you—that is, that we may be mutually encouraged by each other's faith, both yours and mine" (Rom. 1:11–12). Paul desired to bless them with his spiritual gifts. But Paul, the same Paul who wrote most of the New Testament and is perhaps the most godly Christian to ever live, also expected to be blessed *by them*. These ordinary believers at Rome could encourage an apostle.

As you meet with more mature believers God will use *you* to help *them* grow.

- God will use your questions to challenge them.
- God will use your fresh insights to instruct them.
- God will use your zeal to inspire them.
- God will use your prodding to draw them to depend upon him.
- God will use your failures to stretch them.
- God will use your growth to encourage them.

Third, get involved. Don't just be a spectator at church. Can you show up early to serve or meet visitors? Can you stick around after service to talk with people? Does your church have an evening service you can attend? Are there small groups to join? Getting involved provides opportunities to develop discipling relationships, particularly with those who may be able to help you in the ways you hope to grow. Plugging into church life looks different in every congregation, so ask a pastor in your church how to get started.

Fourth, talk with your pastors. Good pastors love to feed hungry sheep. The pastors of your church may not be able to personally disciple you, but they can help you find someone who will. Part of a pastor's job is "to equip the saints for the work of ministry" (Eph. 4:12). Pastors labor to ensure church members can disciple one another, so make yourself known to yours. They can likely connect you with disciplers.

Watch People's Faith

As you spend time in the local church, observe how the believers around you follow Jesus. Hebrews 13:7 encourages us to "Remember your leaders, those who spoke to you the word of God. Consider the outcome of their way of life, and imitate their faith." Watch for people who radiate the life of Jesus and spend time with them. Their godliness will inspire you to imitate them as they imitate Jesus (1 Cor. 11:1). What qualities should you be watching for? Here are a few.

Quality 1: Faithful not Famous. Mama Ruth was a ninety-nine-year-old widow in a nursing home. On the day we met, her wheelchair was parked by a window, and her eyes seemed mesmerized by something outside. I knelt beside her chair. Her wrinkled face turned toward mine. Without any introduction she said: "When I first came to this place, I was very sad. I thought God couldn't use me anymore. But one day while I was sitting here feeling sorry for myself, the Lord reminded me that we shouldn't worry because if God feeds the birds, he will take care of us. So I thought to myself, *Maybe I can help God feed the birds*."

After each meal, Mama Ruth collected left-over bread from the residents' plates. When

people asked what she was doing, she invited
them to join her. She'd wheel over to the door
and have someone throw the bread into the
courtyard. She then parked her chair to see the
birds receive their promised bread. As they did,
she would tell anyone in earshot that this pic-
tured exactly how God treats his children. He
always cares for them, just like he promised he
would.

Mama Ruth taught me how to be faithful
wherever God places me, even if no one notices.
She was not famous in this world, but I trust
things will be different in the world to come.

Quality 2: Wise in the Word. I served on a
church staff with Zach for two years. We ministered together, worked out together, and he
cut my hair in the church basement. He didn't
know it at the time, but he was discipling me.
Zach was a Bible guy. He didn't always carry
his Bible, but you could tell he'd been reading
it. Scripture shaped his entire life. His counsel
was saturated with the word. When he encouraged or corrected me, he did so by pointing
me to Scripture.

I'd been around folks who knew their Bible, but Zach was different. He knew it in a way that made me want to read the Bible and study, not so I could know more than he did, but so I could help people follow Jesus the way he helped me.

Quality 3: Available to Others. Mercury is a town manager near Washington, DC. He loves his wife and spends time with her each evening. He spends one-on-one time with each of his eight children every week. And on top of that, he disciples over twenty men from our church. How does he do that? He uses nearly every lunch hour to meet up with someone to talk about their walk with Jesus.

Mercury opens the word with them, asks tough questions about their personal holiness, helps adjust their family budget, and just about anything else they need to help them honor the Lord. Mercury stewards his time so that he can be available for people who want to grow. And what does he do if he can't fit someone in? He connects them with someone else he has discipled. Mercury has one of the most important traits of a good discipler: he's available.

Quality 4: Evangelistic Outlook. Karen shows up at church hungry to hear from God. But she rarely shows up alone. She almost always brings non-Christian friends. She wants them to believe in the Jesus who transformed her life. She looks for opportunities to talk about Jesus everywhere she goes. Whether at work, with her neighbor, at the gym, or at a local community event—Karen believes God arranges opportunities for her to meet people and point them to Jesus.

Though a relatively young Christian, Karen's evangelistic zeal is contagious. When I hear her pray for the lost, I'm instructed. When she asks questions about how to share her faith, I'm challenged. Find people in your church like Karen who model how to share the gospel with others and inspire you to follow their examples.

I could tell more stories of people who have modeled courage, gentleness, prayer, joy, service, and hospitality—among many other Christlike qualities.[2] No one will perfectly embody every quality of godliness, but keep your eyes open for people who exhibit inspiring faith in Christ. Spend time with those people. Listen to them pray. Observe how they parent. Watch how they evangelize. Ask them questions about the Bible. Follow them as they follow Jesus.

Ask Someone

Don't wait for a more mature believer to pursue you. Pursue them. Take the first step, even if it's intimidating. You'll be shocked to find just how willing and eager mature Christians are to disciple others.

What should you say? It may seem awkward to ask someone to disciple you, but God will give you courage. Approach them at church, give them a call, or write them a note. Invite yourself into their life. Ask them if you can take them out for coffee or grab a meal together. Let them know you are trying to grow in your walk with God and that you've been encouraged by their faith. Share what you've noticed and why you'd like them to invest in you. Tell them if you're hoping to get something specific out of your discipling relationship. Let them know you want to learn how to read the Bible, how to pray, how to better steward your time, how to evangelize, or if you just want to grow in your walk with Christ.

What if you get rejected? "I'd love to, but I don't have the bandwidth to meet with you right now." Jasmine was struck to her core when she received that answer. She'd prayed, she'd planned, she'd gotten her hopes up—and then the person she asked to help her grow with Jesus turned her down. It made her want to quit and go back to just getting by.

Getting turned down is difficult. If someone is unable or unwilling to invest in you, remember that God has not given up on you. His eternal purpose is to conform you to the image of Jesus (Rom. 8:29). He will provide what you need to grow in another way. A friend of mine often wisely reminds me "rejection is just redirection!" If a door shuts with one person, prayerfully pursue someone else. God will use the process to shape you and further mature your faith. And remember, God placed you in a local church so you can pursue discipling relationships with lots of people. If someone in your church can't make time to disciple you, consider building relationships with other folks in your church.

How Do I Make the Most of Discipling Relationships?

As you begin developing a discipling relationship, do your part to make the most of it. Consider these qualities and strive to cultivate them.

Be Prayerful

Pray for yourself (Matt. 26:41). Pray for your church (3 John 2). Pray for the person discipling you (1 Thess. 5:25). Pray, pray, pray. Prayer orients your life toward God. Regular prayer will keep your discipling relationship in proper perspective. Your discipler is not your ultimate hope or help, God is.

Be Reading

Discipling relationships can help you grow, but they don't have power to change you. Only God's word does that (2 Tim. 3:16–17; Heb. 4:12).

Make sure your discipling relationships are centered on the word. If you're struggling to understand Scripture, keep at it. Write down your questions and discuss them with your discipler.

Be Flexible

Your discipling relationships may not turn out as you envision. You're entering another person's life with all of its ups and downs, ebbs and flows. You may only get time with your discipler once or twice a month. What you do together will often vary as well. You may study a book of the Bible, memorize Scripture, read a theological book, do evangelism, or focus on fighting a particular sin pattern. Be willing to flex and trust the Lord's provision for this particular relationship.

Furthermore, the person investing in you may be in a different life stage so you may need to find creative of ways of entering into his or her world. For instance, my wife enjoys discipling. When she was single or newly married, she was available to meet with women in any number of settings. But now, we have five young children. Her life stage significantly limits her availability. Hour-long coffee talks over Romans aren't realistic for her anymore.

In this season, my wife's discipling schedule simply looks different. Sisters who want to spend time with my wife jump into her routine. They talk while folding laundry, join her for grocery shopping, ride along for school pick-up, or hang out with her on nights when I meet with other pastors. The more flexible a sister can be, the more likely my wife will be able to invest in her.

If there's someone you desire to disciple you, do whatever you can to make it easy on the discipler.

- Could you drive to meet for breakfast or lunch near his or her house or place of employment?
- Are there ways you can serve their family in order to get time with him or her?
- Can you carpool on the commute home from work?
- Is there an opportunity to live with a godly family or a more mature believer?

Be Specific

As I said earlier, a lot of discipling relationships emerge naturally as you build relationships with others in your local church. But sometimes you might need help with a particular issue. Clarifying expectations with a discipler will enable them to make a more intentional investment in your life. Some specific requests might sound like this:

- Could we meet for a semester so you can teach me how to study the Bible?
- Could we read the Gospel of John together so I can learn more about Jesus?
- My family is struggling; would you help me think about how to honor them in this season?
- I'm a new parent and I feel lost; would you share some parenting wisdom with me?
- I don't know how to evangelize people; can you take me to share the gospel with someone?
- Can we meet monthly to talk about how I can honor God at work and think biblically about career opportunities?

Again, as you make these requests, don't feel obligated to be discipled by one person forever. Meet with lots of people. You'll need to learn different lessons in different seasons, and you'll often need different disciplers for different issues.

Be Persistent

If you desire to meet with someone, persist in reaching out to them. Guard your heart from resentment if someone feels "too busy" for you. The simple fact is that they may be too busy to meet with you.

Sometimes, however, someone may genuinely desire to invest in you, they just need some gentle reminders. Of course, there's a fine line between persistent and pesky. Be straightforward with them. Simply say, "If it would be better for me to get time with someone else, please just let me know."

You also need persistence to continue developing relationships once previous relationships end. For instance, my church is extremely transient. In a year, as much as a third of our membership may relocate. Members often develop discipling relationships that last only a limited time. As they can attest, continually initiating new relationships can be wearisome. But we must persist. Jesus wants us to be discipled and to disciple others. No matter what challenges you face, continue pursuing discipling relationships in your church.

Be Patient

It may take some time to find the right people to disciple you. Use your time of waiting to invest in others. Keep praying. Keep reading. Keep serving. Don't assume that if you don't find a specific person to disciple you within the next month you can't grow as a Christian.

John Newton, the author of the song "Amazing Grace," once said, "All shall work together for good: everything is needful that he sends; nothing can be needful that he withholds."[3] God is a good Father. He will give us what we need, when we need it. If he hasn't given it yet, it means we

don't need it. This includes discipling relationships. Keep trusting, God is faithful.

Ask Questions

Greg grew up in the Bronx. He hustled on the
streets, spent time in jail, and journeyed through
detox. But Jesus rescued Greg. Since his conversion, Greg has become a relentless question-asker.
Everything about Jesus is new to him. Earlier this
week, I picked him up and he said to me, "So G, I
was reading Hebrews, and I just don't get it, man.
Tell me, what should I be seeing?"

Greg's inquisitive spirit helps him grow as a
Christian, and I encourage you to emulate his
example. When you meet with someone, don't
expect your discipler to do all the work. Learn
to ask questions. Don't worry about having im-
pressive questions, have real ones.

As you read Scripture or listen to a sermon,
write down questions. If you hear a theological
word you don't recognize, ask what it means.
If you see something at church that confuses
you, ask what is happening. Ask questions about

singleness, dating, marriage, raising children. Ask how to steward your time and money. Ask God to cultivate curiosity in your heart about how his word applies to every area of your life. Bring those questions to others, and it will help both of you grow in Christlikeness.

Invite Questions

Discipling requires vulnerability. If you want to grow, you must give people access to your life. Don't share everything with everyone (Prov. 18:24), but a healthy discipling relationship invites inquiry.

I struggled with transparency for much of my early Christian life. I was so worried with impressing my mentors that I avoided being truly honest with them about my sin. Sadly, I was able to deceive and manipulate my way through those relationships for several years until it caught up with me. God graciously rescued me from burying my sin and taught me to bring it before others.

If the person you meet with doesn't ask you pointed questions about your sin, encourage them to hold you accountable for specific sins. Over the years I've learned to help others help me. Below are the kinds of questions I've encouraged friends and mentors to ask me:

- How are you serving your family, especially when you're busy or tired?
- How are you guarding yourself against accessing pornographic material on the Internet?
- How are you intentionally spending time with people who don't know Jesus?
- When was the last time you shared the gospel with someone, and how did it go?
- How are you honoring God with your money? Are you being generous or greedy?
- Is there anyone you find yourself envying? Is there anyone you are bitter toward?
- What provokes you to anger, and how are you responding?

Receive Correction

One of the most sobering commands in the Bible is "do not be deceived" (1 Cor. 15:33; Gal. 6:7; James 1:16). Sin deceives us. It sabotages our relationship with God and saps our joy. We need other believers to help us see the sin we can't see by ourselves. My friend Mark says that discipling is like throwing paint on the invisible man.[4] The more time we spend with someone, the more our sin will be exposed. God uses mature believers to help us recognize and repent of sin we may not be aware of.

Receiving correction is hard but necessary. Just consider how seriously the author of Hebrews warns his readers about the need for correction:

> Take care, brothers, lest there be in any of you an evil, unbelieving heart, leading you to fall away from the living God. But exhort one another every day, as long as it is called "today," that none of you may be hardened by the deceitfulness of sin. (Heb. 3:12–13)

It may not feel like it in the moment, but it's gracious and loving for someone to show us our sin and exhort us toward holiness.

When David concealed his adultery and murder, Nathan confronted him, which led to David's repentance (2 Sam. 12:1–14; Psalm 51). When Peter confused people about the gospel by acting hypocritically at a church picnic, Paul confronted Peter which led to his repentance (Gal. 2:14). I have had the privilege of seeing many brothers and sisters spared from the devastating effects of sin because someone had the concern and courage to confront them about it.

Are you willing to be corrected? Even more, do you *desire* to be corrected?

Fools are marked by resisting correction (Prov. 12:1), but those who receive it gain wisdom (Prov. 15:32). If you want to follow Jesus, you must be willing to receive correction.

Adjust Expectations

Discipling relationships will rarely look exactly like you expect. You may envision the Lord providing you with an intense, one-on-one relationship with a patient, older saint who wisely answers your questions and intuitively anticipates your spiritual needs. More often, you'll find yourself being discipled by a brother or sister you find a bit too abrupt, socially awkward, or scatterbrained. The church is made up of redeemed sinners. Even the godliest among us have faults. If you aren't careful, you can become frustrated when you discover that your discipling relationships are flawed.

To help adjust your expectations, here are a few considerations to keep in mind.

First, your discipler won't be perfect. I often tell folks I'm discipling that they should watch my life and find things they want to emulate and things they want to avoid. I will say and do things they will be encouraged by. They should strive to replicate those qualities. I will also say and do things they will be put off by. They should feel free to correct me and learn from my mistakes. Your discipler will be many things, but perfect isn't one of them.

Second, your discipler won't be God. The people you meet with can't be everything you need. They won't always be available. But Jesus promised, "I [will be] with you always" (Matt.

28:20). They won't be able to do everything for you. But the Holy Spirit is the Helper who gives us power to do all God commands (John 14:16; Acts 1:8). They won't know everything. But God "your Father knows what you need before you ask him" (Matt. 6:8). Brothers and sisters can point you to God, but they can't be God for you. Avoid idolizing those you learn from and allow their inadequacies to point you to the limitless sufficiency of your God.

Third, your discipler can't be the church. No one person can take the place of the local church. You don't just need one member of the body; you need the whole body. God has designed the entire church to play a part in shaping you. Press into many different relationships in your church. Every one of your fellow brothers and sisters has something to teach you.

Fourth, your discipler won't always be impressed. I'm sure Peter was a little surprised when Jesus called him Satan. Hopefully you won't get called Satan, but you will get corrected when you're wrong. The people who disciple you won't always think your insights are amazing.

But don't live for their approval. As Charles Spurgeon once said, "If any man thinks ill of you, do not be angry with him. For you are worse than he thinks you to be."[5] Remember, you don't need to be awesome. Jesus is awesome, not you.

Three Final Encouragements

The longer I'm involved in discipling relationships, the more I realize how much I need God's wisdom. Discipling relationships provide wonderful opportunities for spiritual growth. But you should watch out for a few pitfalls.

Consider Gender Carefully

Just like in a family, brothers and sisters in the local church can spiritually benefit from one another. We find this pattern throughout Scripture. Jesus instructed Mary while she sat at his feet (Luke 10:38–42). Lydia hosted and ministered to Paul (Acts 16:14–15). Priscilla and Aquila corrected Apollos (Acts 18:24–28). The church has always been filled with men and women who edify one another.

At the same time, we need to remember that discipling relationships often create deep and intimate spiritual bonds between two people. Sharing scriptural insights and heart felt prayer requests cultivates spiritual affection. Members of the opposite sex can easily become emotionally entangled in ways that distract from the goal of discipling. If attraction grows, it could lead to hurt, preoccupation with romantic feelings, or even sinful compromise. While we should love and build up both our brothers and sisters in the church, we should also labor to avoid confusing relationships. Thus, it's generally wise to cultivate discipling relationships only with someone of the same gender as yourself.

In fact, Scripture presents a pattern of men focusing their discipling efforts on other men and women focusing on helping other women. For instance, Paul instructs Titus that older women should instruct younger women (Titus 2:3–5). Paul's pattern of discipling primarily included men like Barnabas, Timothy, Titus, Silas, and Luke, among other men. When we observe Jesus's ministry, we find that his twelve disciples were men. Scripture sets forth a pattern of cultivating discipling relationships among people of the same gender.

Intentionally Diversify Relationships

I grew up in a town where everyone looked like me, talked like me, thought like me, voted like me, and experienced life in the same way I did. After I became a Christian, the churches I attended were similar. Everyone shared the same cultural heritage. We sang familiar songs, enjoyed similar preaching styles, and our fellowships reflected our culture.

Years later, I moved to a city marked by extraordinary diversity and began to worship Jesus alongside people quite different than me. As I developed discipling relationships with people from different ethnicities, cultures, social statuses, and economic spheres, my faith matured in unexpected ways. I discovered patterns of sin in my heart I had never previously recognized. I learned to love people who shared little in common with me. The Lord increased my sympathy for suffering friends. I grew to appreciate the beauty of different cultures and preferences.

I share this story because I'm challenging you to seek out discipling relationships with people who are different from you. God will use your differences to teach you to love in meaningful ways. The kingdom of God is made up of people from every tribe, language, and nation (Rev. 7:9). As much as possible, our discipling relationships should be as well.

You may live in an area without much ethnic diversity, but your church likely has folks from different cultural backgrounds, economic situations, and political affiliations. Every local church has old and young, married and single, simple and sophisticated—all bowing before Jesus. The more time you spend with people who experience life differently than you, the more you will see the grace of God shine through them in compelling ways.

As you are able, meet with someone who is different from you. Ask God to give you humility and patience as he uses your differences as instruments to shape you into the image of Jesus.

Process Disappointment Prayerfully

People will fail you. No matter who is discipling you, he or she will eventually let you down. He may not return your text. She may forget a meeting. He may not follow up on that important burden you shared. Some may even end up walking away from Jesus. Experiencing disappointment can tempt you to despair. Here are a few things to remember.

First, Jesus is working on them too. Though it feels like a mature believer should always model godliness, remember that God is maturing them too. A friend of mine always reminds me, "Jesus is always sanctifying everyone at the same time." Just consider how the Gospels show how Jesus is constantly at work in everyone's life. In the span of just a few verses, we find Jesus ministering to a sick person, teaching his disciples a lesson, reproving hypocrites, and calling the crowds to believe. Jesus is amazing like that. Remembering this will enable you to extend patience and forgiveness when others let you down.

Second, Jesus will never fail you. Everyone in this life will let you down. No one is perfect—no one but Jesus. The author of Hebrews reminds us, "Be content with what you have, for he has said, 'I will never leave you nor forsake you.' So, we can confidently say, 'The Lord is my helper; I will not fear; what can man do to me?' . . . Jesus Christ is the same yesterday and today and forever" (Heb. 13:5–8).

Jesus never changes. He was faithful when he called you, and he will be faithful to keep you. Jesus will never lie to you. He will never overlook you. He will never neglect you. He will never betray you. He will never misunderstand you. Allow the failures of others to help you look to Jesus as your ultimate hope.

Let's Get to Work

David felt like he was continually overlooked. He had long desired someone to show him how to be a godly man. Mentors had come and gone, but he never felt like anyone took a serious interest in him. He prayed about it and asked people for help, yet relationships didn't develop like he'd hoped. When he shared his frustration with an older pastor, he received this counsel, "Be for others what you wish someone would have been for you."

That advice changed David's life. Rather than falling into self-pity, he began helping other men navigate their walk with God. He often felt like he didn't know what he was doing, but he prayed for wisdom, and God always seemed to supply what he needed. David still sought advice and encouragement from more mature believers, but he didn't allow his disappointment to keep him from obeying Jesus's command to make disciples.

If you feel overlooked, ask God to help you be for others what you wish someone would be for you. Seek out younger believers and invest in them. Ask the questions you wish someone would ask you. Follow up on conversations in ways you would want someone to do for you. As Jesus said, "Whatever you wish that others would do to you, do also to them" (Matt. 7:12).

I hope this book encourages you to build many relationships with saints who can help you follow Jesus. But remember, fellow believers in your church are looking for someone to disciple them too. Search them out and help them grow in their walk with God. You may feel ill-equipped to do this work, but you are not alone. Jesus promised, "I am with you always, to the end of the age" (Matt. 28:20). No matter how alone or unprepared you may feel, Jesus will be with you, and he will help you.

When Discipling Shall Be No More

Discipling relationships have on the horizon the hope of heaven. Everything we do or discuss in these relationships should be done with the last day in view. Embracing an eternal perspective sobers us, enables us to fight sin, and causes us to cling to God's promises. Our goal in discipling is to help each other follow Jesus until that day when discipling will be no more. The day of Jesus's return is drawing near. Commit your life to helping others make it home.

Recommended Resources

Mark Dever, *Discipling: How to Help Others Follow Jesus* (Wheaton, IL: Crossway, 2016).

Bobby Jamieson, *Growing One Another: Discipleship in the Church* (Wheaton, IL: Crossway, 2012).

J. Garrett Kell, *Pure in Heart: Sexual Sin and the Promises of God* (Wheaton, IL: Crossway, 2021).

Eugene Peterson, *A Long Obedience in the Same Direction: Discipleship in an Instant Society* (Downers Grove, IL: InterVarsity Press, 2019).

J. C. Ryle, *Thoughts for Young Men* (Edinburgh, Scotland: Banner of Truth, 2015).

Ed Welch, *Side by Side: Walking with Others in Wisdom and Love* (Wheaton, IL: Crossway, 2015).

Notes

1. Personal stories involving other individuals are shared in this booklet with permission from those individuals. Often pseudonyms have been used for privacy.
2. For helpful lists of qualities to look for in others, study these passages: Galatians 5:22–23; 1 Timothy 3:1–13; and Titus 1:5–9; 2:1–10.
3. John Newton, *The Works of John Newton*, ed. Richard Cecil (London: Hamilton, Adams & Co., 1824), 2:147.
4. Mark Dever, "4 Ways to Make Disciples," TGC website, May 30, 2016, https://www.thegospelcoalition.org/article/4-ways-to-make-disciples/.
5. Charles Spurgeon, "David Dancing before the Ark Because of His Election" (sermon, Metropolitan Tabernacle, London, July 1, 1888), https://www.spurgeon.org/resource-library/sermons/david-dancing-before-the-ark-because-of-his-election/#flipbook/.

Scripture Index

IX 9Marks

Building Healthy Churches

9Marks exists to equip church leaders with
a biblical vision and practical resources
for displaying God's glory to the nations
through healthy churches.

To that end, we want to see churches
characterized by these nine marks
of health:

1. Expositional Preaching
2. Gospel Doctrine
3. A Biblical Understanding of
   Conversion and Evangelism
4. Biblical Church Membership
5. Biblical Church Discipline
6. A Biblical Concern for
   Discipleship and Growth
7. Biblical Church Leadership
8. A Biblical Understanding
   of the Practice of Prayer
9. A Biblical Understanding and
   Practice of Missions

Find all our Crossway titles
and other resources at
9Marks.org.